Stop Smoking

An Effortless Methodology For Cessation Of Cannabis
Consumption Minimising Negative Effects

*(Cessation Of Smoking: Strategies, Recommendations, And
Strategies For Smoking Cessation)*

Florin Weigl

TABLE OF CONTENT

MORE CAN BE GAINED THAN LOST 1

The Financial, Health, and Social Tolls of Smoking 9

What Causes You to Develop a Smoking Addiction? 19

What is Nicotine Addiction? 24

Make Use of Affirmations to Stay On Course 61

MORE CAN BE GAINED THAN LOST

Many people feel that giving up smoking will be a significant loss in their lives and find it frightening to think about a world without cigarettes. The truth is that quitting smoking will open your eyes to a whole new world of activities, rather than just sipping coffee and puffing on a cigarette. There are actually a lot more benefits to quitting smoking.

To begin with, you will probably notice an improvement in your taste buds and an increase in your ability to smell. You will also be able to enjoy a wider range of foods and beverages that you may not have enjoyed when smoking. I had to change my eating habits when I first started trying to stop smoking; I had to eat more and set a goal for myself—a post-smoking objective. When you give it some thought, you are actually not quitting smoking. It is more important that you create new opportunities for yourself by opening doors.

Allow me to share a little bit of my story with you. Since quitting smoking 180 days ago, I have been focusing on improving my physique and fitness level. I have gained 25 pounds of muscular mass. People at work have been asking me how I achieved it. What keeps me so secret? I merely told them that it was really simple for me to stop smoking right away. I paid no money at all to have someone give me advice on how to stop. You should make it; I made it.

YOU DO NOT USE TOBACCO

You would have to concede to the inevitable after smoking your final cigarette a few months from now. It's a truth of life: mistakes would happen. Realizing this requires conscious effort on your part. There might be situations when, after abstaining from smoking for a few months, you start smoking again.

This can occur if you are exposed to any of the following smoking triggers: tension, worry, or excitement. These feelings have the potential to reverse your gains and push you back towards the habit. . All you have to do is consume that one cigarette and move on. Just stop there and go on. AVOID RETURNING TO THE HABIT! Repeat this: "I don't smoke."

We may have grown more dependent on cigarettes at some time after we first lit one, but I'm positive that none of us were born smokers. Some began in their teens, some in their 20s or 30s, and some as recently as yesterday or an hour ago.

All of us, however, have one thing in common: none of us were born smokers, and it is totally up to you whether or not you want to continue smoking. It's all up to you to decide how free you want to be; I won't stop you from doing so. A smoker and a non-smoker do, however, have one thing in common: neither one of them smoked at birth.

5: Overview and Advice

Secondhand smoke, which is the smoke from a smoker's cigarette that is breathed by loved ones, coworkers, and other people, is also harmful to smokers.

Up to 300,000 instances of pneumonia and bronchitis in infants under the age of eighteen months are linked to secondhand smoke each year.

Parental cigarette smoke increases a child's risk of middle ear problems, aggravates asthma symptoms, and induces coughing and wheezing.

Adolescents who have two smoking parents are over twice as likely to smoke as young people whose parents do not smoke. Young people are also more prone to start smoking in households with just one smoking parent.

The Data

Getting ready to give up

Set a date for your resignation. Try to talk a friend or acquaintance out of smoking with you.

Take note of when and how you smoke. Try to identify the daily activities that you usually engage in while smoking

Change the way you smoke: Store your cigarettes somewhere else. Use the other hand to smoke. Nothing else should be done while smoking. Consider your feelings while you smoke.

Wait a few minutes if you want a smoke. Try to come up with something to do instead of smoking; you may have a glass of water or chew gum.

At a time, buy one pack of cigarettes. Change to a cigarette brand that you find objectionable.

The Financial, Health, and Social Tolls of Smoking

Smoking has a cost that goes beyond daily spending; it can also result in higher costs for health and disaster preparedness, as well as higher costs for medical services due to infections brought on by smoking.

Money Outlays

For some people, smoking can be expensive; these stories may encourage you to give it up. Assuming you smoke two packs of cigarettes a day, you are paying about $400 a month if you spend an average of $7 every bunch of cigarettes in Washington State! (By increasing $14 per day by 28 days in a single month, that is). That's an automobile payment, an airline ticket, or box seats to a Seahawks game; finally, that's extra money in your pocket, provided you're not spending it on smokes.

In addition, there are additional costs associated with health and disaster preparedness for smokers. Because of the higher risk of developing actual chronic illnesses and the higher cost of care over the course of their lifetime, smokers are considered to be higher risk candidates for these types of protection.

Financial Burden of Smoking on You and Your Family

Smoking may have an impact on your family's records. You would agree with me that the money you spend on cigarettes each day would be better used for more essentials like clothing, shoes, and food, or for other items of substantial value. Having a little extra money is also important for those small pleasures that families look forward to, such as a movie night, an outing, or a nice dinner. It's quite likely that smokers experience greater financial strain than non-smokers, and this is especially true if your family has low incomes.

Costs, both material and social

The cost of cigarettes is not only a financial burden; it also affects your health, other people's health, and the stability of society. Handed-down cigarette smoke (SHS) affects everyone in your immediate vicinity; friends, family, coworkers, and your community are among the people it usually harms. One common misconception is that secondhand smoke from cigarettes isn't quite as harmful as actual smoking; in fact, secondhand smoke can be just as dangerous as regular smoke. Natural tobacco smoke (ETS), often known as handed-down cigarette smoke, is a blend of two types of smoke from a cigarette:

• Side-stream: The smoke that escapes the lit end of the cigarette and includes a larger concentration of disease-causing specialists (agents that cause cancer) than standard smoke. • Standard: The smoke that is inhaled directly by the smoker from the cigarette. Additionally, these cancer-causing compounds are smaller particles than those found in regular smoke, which allows them to more easily enter the lungs.

The majority of the smoke that non-smokers experience in a smoky room is side-stream smoke, which accounts for 85% of the ETS.

The U.S. National Toxicology Programme, the International Agency for Research on Cancer, and the U.S. Environmental Protection Agency have organised handed-down cigarette smoke (SHS) as a "known human cancer-causing agent". Cellular degeneration in the lungs, childhood leukaemia, and tumours of the larynx, throat, mind, bladder, rectum, stomach, and bosoms have all been linked to SHS. SHS has also been linked to a variety of illnesses and deaths. Each year in the United States alone, SHS is responsible for approximately 46,000 deaths from heart disease among nonsmokers, 3,400 deaths from lung cellular breakdown in nonsmokers, up to one million children with worsening or newly diagnosed asthma, and between 150,000 and 300,000 lung and bronchus diseases in children under the age of eighteen. In addition, SHS bears financial responsibility for about $10 billion in increased clinical care costs resulting from SHS-related illnesses and deaths.

Habit; explanations for the difficulty in quitting smoking (the highly habit-forming nature of nicotine)

It can be difficult to stop smoking for two reasons:

1. Your brain requires time to adjust to life without nicotine.

2. You must adjust to daily routines that do not include smoking ever again.

It takes time for your mind to adjust to life without nicotine.

Nicotine is the highly addictive substance found in tobacco that makes quitting extremely difficult. The purpose of cigarettes is to rapidly deliver nicotine to your brain.

•Nicotine triggers the emergence of artificial chemicals in your brain that improve your mood. Your brain grows acclimated to nicotine when it repeatedly energises certain areas of your consciousness.

*Nicotine alters the way your mind functions over time, making it seem as though you need nicotine desperately to feel okay.

*When you stop smoking, your brain becomes irrationally angry. You might then experience restlessness or frustration. You might find it difficult to focus or fall asleep, experience strong cravings to smoke, or just generally feel uncomfortable.

*We refer to these feelings as withdrawal. This becomes better about two weeks after you stop, as your brain adjusts to life without nicotine.

*Certain medications used to help people stop smoking include nicotine. This provides you with a safe way to adjust to not having as much nicotine from cigarettes in your brain. Did you know, at least in part, that nicotine actually alters your perception?

You must get used to daily routines that don't include smoking ever again.

• You have a busy schedule that you combine with smoking. When you finally give up, it could be challenging for you to follow these routines without a cigarette in your hand.

- A lot of people link smoking to activities they perform during the day, like taking breaks, sipping coffee, finishing dinner, conversing with friends, or using the phone. These are referred to as triggers. Emotions can also arouse a desire to smoke. You may experience cravings when you start to feel depressed or anxious, or in any case, when you're feeling free or happy. One of these feelings may then trigger the want to smoke when you finally give up.When you finally give up, you'll figure out a way to go through your routine without smoking. Additionally, you'll figure out a non-smoking method of dealing with anxiety or depression.Thankfully, a great deal of people have permanently quit smoking, and the majority say they feel better after a while.

In order to successfully quit, you must handle these two challenges: your mind's addiction to nicotine and your daily routine's inability to smoke cigarettes. Managing both right away could prove to be challenging:

• Quit smoking medications help with the primary exam by reducing cravings and withdrawal symptoms, such as irritability and trouble sleeping or concentrating.

This allows you to focus on the next task: figuring out how to finish the day by engaging in all of the activities you linked with smoking. The good news is that there are many simple things you can do to make it easier, such as finding healthy cigarette alternatives, keeping yourself busy, and controlling your cravings.

What Causes You to Develop a Smoking Addiction?

Nicotine, the substance that leads to dependence, is found in tobacco products, including cigarettes. Researchers have found that nicotine has the same addictive qualities as heroin, cocaine, and alcohol.

Since smokers typically become hooked to unique mixes of stimulants, each smoker's experience and addiction are unique. The addictive qualities of cigarettes that cause smokers to want more are referred to as stimulants.

Your body absorbs nicotine and other substances from cigarettes each time you smoke one. They reach your brain through the bloodstream. Then, they begin to influence your organs, tightening your veins and speeding up your heartbeat and pulse, among other symptoms.

Your neurological system is stimulated by nicotine. This has an impact on your body and brain in many ways.

When nicotine enters your body, adrenaline is released. Your body is stimulated, and your blood pressure and heart rate go up. Additionally, it makes breathing more laborious for you.

Additionally, nicotine causes the release of dopamine, which makes you feel good. This explains why smoking makes you feel calmer. Further, nicotine spreads quickly throughout your brain. This really happens in a matter of seconds.

But after enjoying pleasant feelings, your body deteriorates. Unbeknownst to you, but you really grow tolerant. In order to get the same sense you did previously, you therefore consume more cigarettes. Your tolerance rises with the frequency of your smoking. You develop a compulsive smoking habit.

The Impact of Tobacco

Nicotine affects people both mentally and physically. Among its frequent side effects include headaches, nausea, stomachaches, and dizziness. These effects become more pronounced the longer you smoke. You build up a tolerance to smoking as a habit. This implies that in order to acquire the same results from smoking fewer cigarettes, you will need to use more nicotine.

The body becomes accustomed to a certain amount of nicotine when smoking on a daily basis. Smokers control how many cigarettes they smoke—unknowingly—to keep their blood levels of nicotine at comfortable levels. They may concentrate on the high or pleasure they get from smoking because they are tolerant of the harmful consequences of nicotine. They are unaware that these experiences, which appear to be pleasant, are actually just the body's normal response to nicotine. In actuality, they throw off their bodies' natural equilibrium.

Smoking creates a habit that makes you feel as though you need to smoke to feel normal. You start to feel angry. You find it difficult to concentrate and go about your day without smoking. Additionally, you begin to associate your smoking habit with your everyday activities. This sets off triggers and increases the difficulty of completing your assignments.

For instance, you might connect smoking and coffee use. Thus, you reach for a cigarette every time you get a cup of coffee. Most smokers are unaware of these psychological consequences. A psychological reliance on nicotine develops in them.

When you stop smoking for an extended period, you may experience withdrawal symptoms from nicotine. This is the time when you'll encounter mental and physical adverse effects, such as headaches, agitation, frustration, depression, anxiety, weight gain, trouble concentrating, drowsiness, and trouble sleeping.

The effects of withdrawal may make daily living more challenging. Usually, they start working two hours to two or three days after your last cigarette. However, resist the temptation to revert to your previous behaviors. It is possible to get over these withdrawal symptoms despite the fact that they appear intolerable.

You will discover the methods in this book that can help you beat your addiction to nicotine and permanently stop smoking. You will find the actions you need to perform in order to lessen your withdrawal symptoms from nicotine. Along with learning how to live a smoke-free lifestyle, you will also learn coping mechanisms for your illness.

WhatisNicotine Addiction?

Nicotine is present in all products containing tobacco, and unfortunately, it is straightforward to become addicted to this particular ingredient. When you first start smoking, usually in your mid- or late-adolescent years, you will only be able to light up a few cigarettes in a few days before you begin to build up your nicotine tolerance.

But why is that novel so adversarial?

As you may already be aware, nicotine can aid in relaxing the chemicals that trigger your brain's reversal process.

After you start regularly smoking cigarettes and other tobacco-containing goods, your body's reroute pathway chemistry also changes accordingly. Subsequently, you acquire the programming to search for tobacco products to satiate your cravings, even if you are well conscious of the consequences you will face if you persist in smoking and suppress your desire to quit.

The desire you have to lighten up a little will serve as a reminder to you to raise the level of your nicotine intake in order to prevent the strain and discomfort that are typically associated with nicotine withdrawal symptoms. Because of the rapid effects of nicotine, withdrawal symptoms usually appear a few hours after the drug is stopped. When quitting smoking, you may experience symptoms of nicotine withdrawal, such as intense cravings, difficulty controlling your emotions, restlessness, irritability, anxiety, difficulty sleeping, and depression. If you smoke, your nicotine intake increases. Levels through consistently smoking throughout the day, with the majority of smokers doing so after work.

When you give up smoking, you will experience withdrawal symptoms, but there are some beautiful things in store for you. Most smokers discover that their nicotine withdrawal symptoms usually appear after three or four days, and they typically don't last longer than ten to fourteen days.

Even while you may not feel like it, the truth is that you are actually getting better, and in just two weeks, your system can already be free of the majority of symptoms related to thyroid dysfunction. When this happens, you will be begging people to quit smoking, which will make it easier for you to lead a smoke-free life. Smokers do not typically experience a wide range of symptoms over an extended period.

The good news is that these symptoms can be reduced and, in the case of multiple smokers, can be eliminated entirely with the use of NRT, nicotine replacement therapy, or any other prescription medication meant to treat smoking cessation.

Attend nonsmoking eateries as soon as possible.

Take vitamins to help you quit smoking: a widespread belief among smokers, so until your body and mind begin to benefit from quitting smoking, you should both temporarily abandon your regular schedule.

It takes two hands to light a cigarette; however, those with specialized training need to use one. How about keeping your hands occupied with a pencil and eraser?

Smoking is a highly addictive behavior. As a result, avoid hanging out with smokers and those who beg you to avoid smoking around them.

There are certain moments when smoking is best, such as B. after lunch or tea, when you are most vulnerable to provocation. Why not experiment with methods to stray today for the benefit of yourself? If you want to keep your hands occupied after lunch, you can also plan your task.

You can pass the time by trying churns or toffees. Yixing Non-Smoking Herbal "Cigarettes" are a popular make-believe product that mimics the flavor of actual cigarettes while allegedly being less dangerous than conventional cigarettes.

These are suggested in these phases of smoking cessation. We don't endorse them because we haven't looked into the integrity of their chemical composition or how they affect smokers.

The reasoning behind this is straightforward: in five to seven years, the number might drop to twenty.

It feels like we're merely running in circles once we've deceitfully convinced ourselves that we've discovered a less dangerous addiction. For us, smoking a cigarette might even become an addiction to anything.

Similarities to cigarettes must be entirely outlawed because our weak minds will continue to try to console and justify us as we give in to the allure of smoke in another form.

You should be aware that taunts are fleeting, but desires have the power to make you question your confidence on a deep level. Nicotine boosts your mental state, but it also steadily undermines your self-esteem. Your confidence suffers after you decide to give up. Some people frequently succeed in convincing you by sharing their personal experiences, which causes them to relapse after their initial cessation. The fact that they've taken to smoking cigarettes may be a comfort. Using more extensive filters, as suggested by Larger filter cigarettes, is mistaken for being less dangerous, according to some quacks. Regardless of the size or quantity of filters, we think that smoking cigarettes continues the addiction to tobacco. There are various smoking cessation techniques. The acupuncture technique is among the most organic healing methods. It makes you feel against smoking because of the way it plays with your taste buds. The flavor will deteriorate if you provide it's the first train that you take after acupuncture treatment. We hardly ever advise you to see a doctor for therapy of any type to help you live a simpler life; instead, we insist that you work hard and overcome obstacles on your own. When you can stop taking medicine or receiving treatment for a few days after quitting, we promise you will have unending confidence. You may demonstrate to yourself that you are in control of both your surroundings and your passion.

Given that this is rather general information, it will assist you. Depending on each person's mental capacity, they differ. In addition, we counsel you to examine yourself and determine whether you require outside counseling while paying attention to your inner guidance. Even medical facilities like

Holistic Healthcare Online address its effects even after alternative medicine has given up on them. You can also look into Penn Therapy and hypnosis to assist you in coping with the fallout from being abandoned. As a result, the challenge gets more cerebral.

Weak people may begin to believe that they are no longer helpful and that everything in their environment has grown dull. They may feel let down despite their desperation. Deciding to stop smoking is, therefore, more like a punishment. Another discovery that knocks you sideways is But keep in mind that it becomes more challenging to defend a judgment afterward. So, after you've made the crucial step of being true to a daring decision, why give up? The long-term consequences of nicotine may somewhat impact your energy levels, but you have been spared numerous ailments that may have been fatal.

Have you ever considered the possibility that dizziness is a transient side effect? Regarding yourself, who do you think has the most chance of defeating the dreaded nicotine? Does he not exist on another psychological plane? Be cheerful and think positively. Compute the potential financial reward as one method of optimistic thinking. Do the math now: what was the amount you saved today? Is it $2? After five days, how does the figure look? Thus, you either save a lot for your lifestyle or your family or kids. At least you're using the money for enjoyment rather than burning it. Thus, remind yourself to keep going! We're going to have another great tour in a year! Not joking around, $770

After-Quit Treatments We genuinely think that the most effective treatment for quitting smoking is confidence. We are working with a population that lacks confidence in themselves; they require outside counseling to stop smoking before and after. We think that you need to focus in order to become more motivated. Intrance It is among the first forms of medicine used by earlier societies. In the past, people primarily focused on healing based on inner energy levels in China, Tibet, and India. In the past, individuals were administered cosmic rays as an external energy source to treat medical ailments. For the majority of long-established addictions, hypnosis was the primary form of treatment. It helps alleviate mental suffering in addition to eliminating the necessity of dependence.

In hypnotherapy, the initial stage is to evaluate your susceptibility, which in turn establishes the extent of treatment needed. You can choose to hear a deep voice, focus on moving things, or even see lighting effects. Even today's Western nations are seeing a rise in the use of this therapy. Mindfulness is among the most advanced forms of alternative medicine now used, having been utilized by ancient Chinese or Indian civilizations. In the US and the UK, where it has been shown to be the most effective stress-reduction method, meditation is becoming increasingly authentic. Linked inquiries. Meditating was one of the ways that the ancient gurus connected with God. These days, it helps you become more focused and concentrated while relieving you of external suffering. Smoking increases your susceptibility to the long-lasting emotional effects of nicotine, which merely stimulates your central nervous system. Stressed-out workers should meditate, according to scientific studies. The medical study team has demonstrated that one of the best ways to boost the three primary forces of motivation, self-confidence, and willpower is through meditation. Who is able to battle for the choice to give up smoking? Consuming tobacco.Guidance A Massachusetts General Hospital study demonstrates the value of smoking cessation counseling. After returning home, counseling assists them in quitting.

There were 650 adult smokers involved in the investigation. The American Cancer Society ensures that those who wish to stop smoking permanently can get assistance. The psychological aspect of the addiction is the primary focus of the counseling session. You may even decide to consult over the phone. Releases his and confirms its veracity. Alabama," where the researchers examined more than 16,000 smoking records, is published in the American Journal of Medicine It was discovered that measurable quantities had demonstrated an advantageous impact on patients who were released from the hospital following a heart attack.

Finding the ideal counselor in the area is what you should accomplish in order to arrange some sessions with them. Treatment for Nicotine Replacement If you examine the most dangerous component of cigarettes, it is unquestionably nicotine. Nicotine indeed causes a significant amount of physical dependence, which has been linked to a number of unpleasant symptoms during and even after the smoking cessation phase. Patches, sprays, and inhalers are free of the additional adverse tobacco side effects.

Not only are sunflower seeds crunchy, but they also make an excellent filler.

Dried fruits, such as apricots, cranberries, bananas, raisins, or dried bananas.

Route mix, either premade or something you have actually mixed yourself, is as easy as blending peanuts, raisins, sunflower seeds, a few shredded coconut, and anything else that will provide you with a crunchy and delicious combination.

Low-calorie snacks, which you could either microwave or consider buying a little air popper. These are usually really affordable and can be kept on the counter.

There are several ways that a hypnotherapist or your doctor may help you stop, but perhaps you're still deciding whether to take that route. What specific actions can you take to try to stop on your own and succeed right now?

You may need to make some critical decisions when it comes to occasions like casino poker evenings or other gatherings where it's assumed that everyone else can relax and also lighten up if they so choose. If this is going to someone else's home, keep in mind that while you might request that they be smoke-free right now, doing so does not qualify you to make that request alone.

Examine your list of situations in which smoking is only a natural reaction, and also make a note of other things you may do to avoid that situation, keep your hands occupied, or divert yourself. Consider diaries you could read, music you could listen to, or chores around the house you could complete when you had some free time.

In addition, smoking cigarettes dries out every part of your body since you are unable to get enough oxygen to every aspect of your body. Water rehydrates your cells, which helps to repair this damage.

Yes, chewing gum is also a really effective way to help you stop. Your mouth is busy and engaged, which makes you less inclined to want to smoke.

In addition to being a physical habit that is hard to break, smoking cigarettes is one of the reasons quitting is so difficult. Her mother would force her to go back and complete the task if she didn't, so eventually, she learned to go for the light button the moment she left the house.

Many people are afraid to lose weight, which makes them reluctant to give up smoking cigarettes. Pure nicotine indeed seems to accelerate your metabolism; additionally, after you stop smoking cigarettes, your metabolism often slows down.

There are numerous natural and holistic detoxifiers available. Among the most well-known are, among others:

The fact that you are making an effort to give up cigarettes should be at the top of that list! The idea that smoking cigarettes calms and relaxes you has scientific support. Many people don't know how to relax. Therefore, they need to find alternative ways to decompress besides smoking cigarettes.

We could also provide our bodies with the tools they need to do this. This implies the right amount of fruit, vegetables, fiber, and water.

We could significantly aid our bodies' natural cleaning processes if we abstained from initially exposing them to toxic toxins. This means avoiding convenience foods, which include processed foods, deep-fried foods, and junk food, as these typically include terrible components.

Fennel, or Foeniculumvulgare, has been used since ancient times as a natural appetite suppressor and was frequently used to quell during worship. In addition to its inherent diuretic properties, fennel supports healthy kidney, liver, and spleen function and soothes acid reflux. More recently, fennel has been shown to help relieve indigestion in general and colic in particular.

The body has mechanisms in place to get rid of harmful substances and other waste products; often, all that's needed is a little help to get this process started.

Natural cleansing.

Taking care of the diet plan has many benefits, and relieving the cravings to smoke is just one of them. There are many organic ways you might clean yourself of these terrible pollutants, regardless of your interest in holistic solutions or your desire to try getting rid of these toxic poisons on your own.

The plant Taraxacumofficinalis, or dandelion, is still grown in many parts of the world today and was traditionally used in Native American medicine. It is made up of bitter ideas that are beneficial to the digestion and liver systems.

Every cigarette smoker will tell you that smoking is about more than just a physical hunger yearning. Is this person genuinely a good friend to you if they are pushing you to keep smoking so they don't feel left out or guilty about their decision to keep smoking cigarettes?

Generations of Khoi/San descendants and Xhosa standard therapists are familiar with Pelargonium reniforme, a medicinal plant known for its health-promoting properties. Known as it is widely used for a variety of therapeutic purposes and is well known for its beneficial effects on liver function and digestive system restoration.

gaining weight after giving up smoking

A lot of people who used to smoke gain weight after they stop. This serves as an excuse for some people to continue smoking. Still, the risks associated with smoking outweigh any slight weight gain. Prioritize maintaining your health when trying to quit by consuming lots of fresh produce, whole grains, healthy fats, and fruits. Be sure to stay hydrated, get enough rest, and exercise.

Include exercise in your everyday routine.

Avoid driving. Take the kids for a stroll or a jog to school and back.

Walk more quickly when mowing the yard.

Quickly complete the housekeeping.

When you get the chance, go swimming.

Never go short distances in the car.

Take the dog for regular walks.

Take a stroll through parks and retail centers.

Walk home after getting off the bus or train one stop early.

Take a quick workout during lunch.

Never use the elevator; always use the steps.

Engage in some modest exercise while you watch TV.

After supper, take a walk with your neighbor, a member of your family, or a friend.

Stress reduction

People who smoke and find it challenging to stop frequently blame stress for their relapses. Both smokers and non-smokers experience stress in their lives; the only distinction is that chronic smokers have adopted a reliance on smoking as a coping mechanism. You may argue that it's a lousy method of stress relief. You must learn new coping mechanisms for stress if you want to avoid smoking. While NRT or nicotine replacement therapy can be helpful in the short term, you cannot live a life solely dependent on supplements. It would be best if you healthily managed your stress.

Using mindfulness to reduce stress

It promotes making the most of every moment, especially the difficult ones. Mindfulness is an attitude toward healthy living, not only a method of reducing stress. You learn to watch without making any changes when practicing mindfulness.

Maintain a relaxed posture while sitting on a chair or the floor, keeping your back, neck, and head straight but not stiff.

Focus on something commonplace, like breathing. With every breath, concentrate on how the air feels as it enters and exits your body. Avoid attempting to regulate your breathing by going faster or slower. Just watch.

Your thoughts may stray even as you are paying attention to your breathing. Keep an eye on where your thoughts wander, whether it's to a far-off recollection or concern for an upcoming event. Gently bring your attention back to your breathing after observing.

Breathe as a stabilizing anchor. Every time your thoughts stray, pay attention to where they go, acknowledge them for a brief minute, and then go back to breathing.

Increase it gradually to five minutes, then to ten, twenty, or even thirty minutes.

This practical advice, suggestions for losing weight, and methods for handling stress can enable you to quit smoking for good.

Natural Medicines

If you'd prefer not to worry about side effects or poisons, you can try more common, non-traditional methods such as needle therapy, spellbinding, or meditation. Even while there is little logical evidence to support the practicality of these approaches, that doesn't mean one of them can't be effective for you.

In auriculotherapy, for example, explicit focuses on the external ear are stimulated. According to a recent analysis published by the Journal of the

American Leading Body of Family Medicine, it is safe but no more effective than a phony remedy. Concurrently, it has been employed by a skilled professional in one of America's Malignant Growth Treatment Centers, and some people claim to find it to be really beneficial.

Two more safe but dubious methods that some specialists suggest include low-level laser treatment, often known as cold laser treatment, and magnet treatment, which involves placing magnets on the ear. The final option uses lasers in place of needles and is similar to needle therapy.

Natural Medicine

It's unlikely that improved nutrition will help you give up smoking on its own. That being said, when you make the effort to halt, it can undoubtedly strengthen the system of healing. Sound therapy can relieve your body of toxins, repair the health deficiencies common to smokers, and manage the apparent withdrawal symptoms.

• Increase your intake of leafy vegetables, especially the dull green ones like spinach and kale, and the yellow and orange ones like squash, pumpkin, carrots, and yams. These will provide indisputable levels of antioxidant enemies and various nutrients that aid in protecting against some forms of cancerous growth, such as lung cellular degeneration. If you need to give yourself a kick start on your diet, try a five-day water and juice fast, which is a popular strategy used by many people to quit smoking, suggests Balch.

•Speak with your health professional to determine whether you need any extra improvements. For example, increased vitamin E can protect your cells and organs from smoke damage, and more vitamin A can help repair mucous membranes and protect your lungs, according to Balch. Some spices, such as red clover and burdock root, can help flush toxins from the bloodstream, and lobelia and valerian root may help ease the symptoms of withdrawal.

*Natural health experts agree that avoiding certain foods and drinks is essential. These include alcohol, coffee, sugar, and processed foods, all of which might increase your desire to smoke. When you do have to satisfy a craving, try your hand at eating crunchy, healthy snacks like apple slices, carrot sticks, or almonds.

Alternatively, you may stop. Unadulterated and basic

Specific clinical resources warn against stopping abruptly. They advise against withdrawal since it is complicated and claim that those who take medications or NRT are more successful. Some

An online journal paper published in PLOS Medication examines quitting smoking, both with and without assistance. The authors observe that the majority of material circulating on the subject implies that NRT or prescription drugs are necessary for real progress. In any event, data from the American Cancer Society indicates that 90% of smokers who stopped did so on their own. Although the majority of advice given to smokers advises against using this tactic, the article indicates that quitting abruptly is still the recommended course of action.

Dr. Joseph Mercola, who also supports this method, advises starting with eliminating the rest of your wellness tendencies. Make changes to your diet, start exercising, and get enough rest. He thinks that once you've addressed the basic movements towards your well-being, you should give up. Putting your health and well-being first will make quitting easier.

Once more, our health worries are valid, well-supported, and both politically and personally acceptable grounds for giving up. And for similar reasons, millions of smokers have given up. And a lot of them are content and at ease in their new non-smoking lifestyle. Some admit it aloud: "I stopped smoking five years ago, and I've wanted to smoke every day since." individuals who, after stopping for five or ten years, encounter specific difficulties in their lives that ultimately cause them to fall into temptation and start smoking again.

Health-related reasons are valid and should be adequate justifications for quitting, yet they are frequently insufficient. If we base our decision to stop smoking on "physical health reasons," we might actually wait until we are so unwell that we are unable to move our arms or raise our heads off the pillow. We will then give up smoking, at least temporarily, since it will be physically challenging to continue smoking. Till we heal and regain the necessary physical capacity to continue.

Let's take a closer look at what it actually means to give up on health concerns once more.

Physically speaking, as I just mentioned, we can actually keep smoking until we are confined to bed and unable to move our hands or heads. Alternatively, we can keep smoking until the smoke becomes too thick for us to inhale physically.

Therefore, when we declare that we are quitting for "physical health reasons," we are really depending on our mental health, unless and until we are in these exceedingly terrible medical circumstances — when we are literally too sick to smoke.

We are thinking about our current and past health illnesses. We are attempting to leverage our beliefs about being healthy or unhealthy as a means of quitting. When we worry about our health, we project feelings of loss, guilt, and terror into our minds. None of us enjoys thinking about such projections in our minds. We, therefore, shift our focus elsewhere. "I need to do the laundry first, even though I know I should stop because I've been coughing a lot."

In order to successfully employ "health reasons" as a quitting strategy, we must teach ourselves to think about our health—whether it be good or bad—all day, every day, until we stop smoking. Few of us possess the mental self-discipline to focus our attention on a single subject for the entire day on a topic we find boring. Still, this is how a great deal of smokers approach giving up. It is indeed advised for smokers to approach quitting in this manner. Imagine how wonderful you will feel. Recall how miserable you were.

Yes, for a brief while, we can accomplish this. And after a short interval, repeat it once more. It is asking a lot to expect us to do this all day, every day when we already smoke, which we do without thinking. It makes sense why quitting success rates are so low.

Naturally, we can utilize our concerns and the mounting evidence of health issues in our daily lives as a trigger to give up smoking. A lot of smokers have. Furthermore, the conventional justification for abstaining from smoking is "health reasons." However, let's be honest with ourselves: despite being politically correct, giving up on health concerns is actually the most challenging route to take. This hasn't been our experience over a very long period of time.

Adequate said. Alright, let's return to the simple methods of quitting.

We'll examine how smoking—doing our smokes—is clearly a lifestyle as well as an action in the upcoming . We'll discuss how giving up smoking can be a straightforward, clear lifestyle choice that we can all readily and gradually adopt over the course of several days or weeks. Is quitting smoking a way of life?

Junctions

Whenever faced with a decision in life, watch the gangster movie for guidance. The gangster movie has a lot of wise counsel that I have found. There are numerous life lessons in the film about the mobster!

I will direct you to Sean Connery's Untouchables at this very intersection.

Kevin Costner is asked, "What are you prepared to do? What are you willing to offer? At the age of 58, Humphrey Bogart, my teenage hero, passed away from esophageal cancer. I apologize, but I will not be leaving at 58. Grandkids on my knee is what I want. I would rather enjoy my senior years than endure such pain. Even if I do suffer and die from cancer, I want to pass away knowing that I no longer commit suicide. As Bogie lay there, what do you think he was thinking?

Not me, sweetheart! Forget about that! That's not how I'm going out. How about thee? What do you want out of life, and how willing are you to go to achieve your objectives? How do you plan to pay for your future?

Here's a quick task for you:

Write about your future in your journal.

Which dreams do you have? Can you make them become objectives? Could you write what lies ahead?

Present Circumstances

I feel like the real me has returned since I gave up smoking. Either way, smoking does not represent the "real" you or the "real" me. It's ironic that I had to smoke to discover that. I am looking forward to getting old with my wife and having children now that I have a wife. Now, it all seems possible.

Do I overlook it? Of course! Will I return? Not at all! Never do! It's not going to occur. I can't go back because I'm too involved with the here and now. And why would I? The thought of having to quit again serves as a sufficient incentive never to start up again. I occasionally like to smoke a cigar. I'll take it as it comes and smoke in the Bill Clinton fashion—that is, without taking a puff. I become "cool" once more as the romance reappears. After that, for the next twenty-four hours, my tongue tastes like an ashtray, my fingers smell like I gave a cow a proctology exam, and

I'm reminded of all the reasons I stopped doing this in the first place.

I remember not being able to run as fast as I can today or snatch a kettlebell over my head 100 times in five minutes, and I think about that when I see other people smoking. I imagine myself out of breath, the stench of my car, and having to tell people I'm going to smoke so I can spend time with my now-wife or family.

Time is significant, priceless, and irreplaceable once it is used up. Use it carefully.

I feel as though I have entirely circled back. I rebelled and started smoking. I am a rebel, though. The moment I discovered I couldn't operate without smoking, I began to lose interest in smoking. My next cigarette consumed my entire existence, and gradually, it got to be annoying. It bothers me to be so uncontrollably wild. I'm under Big Tobacco's control, bro! I had to stand up to that regime. What they were selling, I purchased. I was hooked, line and sinker for it. Lamps?Light-flavored cigarettes? Who are we kidding? Come on? Merely Us! You're breathing in over 4,000 chemicals, 43 of which are known to cause cancer, so filter or not filter—it doesn't really matter. The term "light cancer" is unfounded.

"Bob, what type of cancer do you have?"

"Oh no, I'm sick with light cancer!"

Could you permit me to unwind? Quit lying to yourself and letting other people profit from your pain and self-medication.

Taking a broad perspective, I observe that many influential individuals in our society want to convince each of us that we have little influence over our lives. That when you make a mistake, you are not to blame. Because you were abused as a child, you are immune from punishment for the abuse you inflict on others. Given that your father cheated on your mother, does it make sense, or is it normal for you to cheat on your wife?

Reality TV is rewarding and glamorizing inappropriate behavior. These rappers are teaching kids that being a "gangsta" is okay and that being a killer or drug dealer is necessary for success. Has effort ever gone unnoticed? Bill Clinton is a great role model to follow, and his wife is the picture of moral rectitude. He betrayed a pledge he made to God; let me tell you that. That is not what you do. And she stays with him as his wife? I mistook her for a feminist. What did America learn? What are our children being taught and taught? If you smoke, what are you teaching your children? Not as I do, but as I say? My relatives used to advise me against smoking. I would receive entire essays explaining why I shouldn't succumb to the smoking trap, with a subtle irony of "could you pass the ashtray" thrown in. Come on, folks! Is it acceptable to make mistakes as long as you sincerely apologize afterward? How is it accomplished? What connection does this have to smoking? Really nothing. What's choosing got to do with it? All of it. That is entirely related to smoking.

Refuse to allow anyone or society to persuade you that you are not in charge. Every moment of your life is under your control. Regardless of the past, your behavior is entirely your own, and only you have the power to choose how you will behave in the future.

Make Use of Affirmations to Stay On Course

SYnopsisWORDsareverypowerful, and if you're looking to continue your journey to break free from the habit, you can be confident that the following statements will help you tremendously.

Positive Phrases for a Successful Conclusion

Even if quitting smoking is difficult, there is one effective strategy you may try: using positive affirmations. Why is that? It's simply because all of your thoughts will help determine how you actually feel, and your sentiments about a particular subject typically trigger the correlating actions.

I love my family and myself more than I love smoking.

I am no longer a smoker, ever.

I say no to smoking and a hearty "yes" to life.

I have complete control over my life.

I look and feel fantastic.

I am free from nicotine and free from nicotine cravings.

I remove the act of smoking from my life.

I prefer life over death.

I refuse to allow smoking to overcome me.

My lungs are healthier, more precise, and cleaner.

I enjoy breathing in clean, fresh air and hate smoking.

I enjoy getting up early every morning because I know that my lungs are cleaner now and that my body is no longer covered in blood vessels.

I smoke from a cigar, and I'm healthy and fit.

I don't react negatively to compliments.

I feel better than ever after giving up smoking—happier, healthier, and more at ease.

Instead of smoking, I chose to take care of my health, happiness instead of depression, and freedom instead of addiction.

Since quitting smoking, my heart has become healthier, my blood pressure has returned to normal, and I have never felt happier.

I'm a calm, relaxed non-smoker.

Every new day pushes me in the direction of becoming healthier and better and keeps me away from smoking.

I am enjoying eating more now that the food is becoming healthier for me.

I feel better now, and other people want to be with me.

I have never felt this content and grateful in my entire life.

My body feels purified and cleansed now.

My body is prepared for toxins.

I have control over my cravings, and the only things I have left are the healthy ones.

These days, I feel younger and healthier.

I am breathing better than ever right now.

10: Advantages Of Sustaining Your Quit Smoking Program

SYnopeiA

Once you break free from your smoking habit, you can anticipate many positive changes in your life. Discover the several benefits that you might expect once you uphold and adhere to your commitment to quit smoking.

Give up smoking and make positive changes in your life.

For some people, quitting smoking may merely be a matter of maintaining one's health, but in actuality, there are many benefits that you may anticipate, encounter, and enjoy once you make a complete commitment to doing so.

Savor a Greater Life Experience

If you want to watch your grandkids grow up and become adults, you must give up smoking as soon as possible. Smoking increases the probability of dying ten times early due to many life-threatening illnesses that are linked to this unhealthy habit.

Reduce Your Risk of Experiencing Various Health Conditions: Smoking cigarettes can put your life and quality of life at risk. There is a significant likelihood that you will deal with ticks every single day. If you want to live a healthy and free life from various illnesses like fertility problems, impotence, macular degeneration, cataracts, osteoporosis, tooth loss, and gum disease, make sure you quit smoking as soon as possible.

Make Your Body Pure Like a Baby's Everybody likes babies, and by suctioning, you also raise your chances of having a body that is identical to a baby's all over again. Give up smoking immediately if you want to feel pure and sound like a baby. When you do this, it will only take a few minutes for you to return to your natural state, which includes your blood pressure, pulse rate, and the natural temperature of your hands and feet.

Give your heart a rest every single night.

You can also contribute to improving your sexual life by taking up smoking. For both genders, it can be very beneficial to stay away from cages. Women will be more easily aroused and will have better erotic experiences.

Above all, the eyes of the other sex will find you more attractive if you don't smoke.

Stop the Harsh Coughing

If you adhere to your quit smoking resolution, you will notice a noticeable decrease in your heavy coughing. Breathing difficulties and shortness of breath will co-occur because your lungs are unable to function normally once more. When your lungs return to normal, it can increase lung function, heal the lungs, and reduce the likelihood of developing various infections.\

3. Aging prematurely One of the key and fundamental reasons why the youngest adult is aging quickly is because they are faced with the problem of smoking. Smoking can cause severe changes to the skin, causing persons who smoke often to have the skin I would term alligator skin. Alligator skin signifies that the smoker's skin gets highly leathery, nearly like a boot. Also, smoking makes people look a lot older than they indeed are. If smokers are weary of not appearing young, they should stop smoking. Smoking makes people look older because the blood vessels in smoker's faces get severely constricted, so blood can't flow normally. Afterward, blood doesn't get to the organs readily, and it comprises the skin, consequently resulting in fast aging. Another clue that a person has been smoking for a long time is that they have stains on their hands from the cigarettes they smoke. This gives their hands a special kind of look that makes it so unappealing. The smoking of the cigarette is more noticeable around the face since we see

proof of smoking from stained skin owing to the tars and the poisons emitted in every smoke. The muscular motions around the mouth are meant to be breathed and exhaled, which would lead to the distinctive smoker's wrinkles around the mouth if not inhaled and expelled.

4. Requirements from the social community as a whole. You can tell if you'll become or remain a smoker by observing the folks you spend time with. You will likely start smoking if the majority of the individuals you spend time with smoke. People are more influenced by being accepted into a social group than we realize. . People frequently hid somewhere to smoke so no one would see them because smoking embarrassed them and made them feel weaker both physically and mentally. Smoking can seriously damage a smoker's self-concept. One of the leading causes of the rapid rise in smoking rates

and the degradation of the social standing of those who like smoking is that, in addition to smokers, many others inhale secondhand smoke, which further exacerbates the health risks associated with smoking. Not only does secondhand smoke worsen the smell of my clothes whenever I go out to buy junk food or any snack, but it also poses a threat to people who are healthy and do not smoke by releasing carcinogens and other substances that are more easily absorbed than firsthand smoke. These are some of the reasons behind the [fair indoor air] constitution.

5. Seeking someone who has knowledge of and access to social media, publications, or who has personally encountered the phrase

6. An addiction to smoking damages the bloodstream, lungs, and vessels. It also makes it harder to find the perfect

companion. News is the primary motivator for teenage boys to abstain from smoking. 7. Diseases are a common occurrence. It's possible that you are aware of the risk that smoking poses, which could ultimately result in death, but you disregarded the advice given. Smoking exposes one to a variety of bacteria and viruses, and the harmful substances that are released into the bloodstream can harm the body's systems. You probably start to bother other people. According to estimates, secondhand smoke results in more than 50,000 fatalities annually.The fact that one puff of tobacco contains over 4,600 compounds, of which over 40 are dangerous, is hardly new information. This increases the risk of vascular obstruction or heart attacks.

9. One of the harmful effects of smoking is the loss of energy and muscle, which makes it extremely difficult to complete even a primary task like walking 0.25 km without breathing heavily. Adolescent athletes who smoke also

suffer from physical ailments and are less active overall since smoking causes the heart and lungs to become less efficient over time.

10. Smoking regularly can have a significant financial and time cost. but generally speaking, packs cost between $5 and $6, and in certain places, that sum can reach $11 when federal and state taxes are taken into account. Because cigarette businesses seek to maximise profits regardless of the potential health risks to their customers, this is incredibly economical. If you live somewhere where a carton of cigarettes costs, say, $6, that's almost $3,000 a year. That ignores the fact that an average smoker uses two to three extra sick days annually, has 7% fewer formative years, and incurs additional health costs of $1,500. As one expert puts it, It is imperative that smokers modify their viewpoint towards smoking. They might start viewing smoking differently, going from thinking it's a beautiful thing to thinking it's a

terrible habit that will ruin my life. If people want to see a significant difference in their lives, they must take this action.

After you've decided on a quit date, you should never forget that you must be entirely ready for that day. There shouldn't be any more turning back, therefore you should exert all of your effort to see your goal through to completion.

You need to know what specific categories people fit into after determining their respective quit dates before you even move on to the next stage. The top three categories are as follows:

Category 1: Those who were highly ill from smoking. They became weary of the lethal routine. The reason they were successful in quitting smoking was that they made the decision never to look back.

Category 2: Sick individuals. They are not necessarily sick from smoking, which sets them apart from those in Category 1. Instead, they are really ill. Usually, their smoking habit is the cause of their ailments. Usually, the conditions are as straightforward as the ordinary flu or smoker's cough. After their experience, they made the decision never to smoke again. Their lives were improved by the three days spent in the hospital bed.

Category 3: The worst category to be in is this one. These are the smokers who receive the dreadful ultimatum from their doctors: stop smoking now or you will die before you know it. However, the smoker has the final say in the matter. These individuals typically have far more complicated medical conditions. If they don't stop, they could actually end up dead because their lives are in danger.

5: Maintain Your Quit Effectively!

Among all the phases in the quitting process, abstaining from smoking is considered the most crucial and last. Numerous techniques are recommended in books and online, but the most outstanding design for you is usually the one that works for you. You must have a deep understanding of who you are as a smoker. To have a wider variety of possibilities, you should also thoroughly investigate all of your selections.

If, after months of stopping, you still feel tempted to smoke, you can try any of the following strategies to help you resist the urge:

*) give the craving time to subside. Occasionally, even long after you've stopped using nicotine, it's pretty natural to experience cravings for a cigarette stick. Rather than being chemical, it might be more of a behavioural phenomenon. If you have been craving something for the last fifteen minutes, consider how much of

your life you can save if you choose to remain abstinent.

*) Think back to all the reasons you wanted to give up. If you have trouble remembering all of your motivations, list them in your journal. Read out loud your justifications each time you feel like smoking again. In this manner, you will be inspired to give up smoking for good.

*) Share your recent struggles with a friend or member of your family. Ideally, it would help if you chose someone who witnessed the entire experience. It will be much easier for you to recall what you gave up in order to lead a better lifestyle if you choose a witness to your experiences.

*) Make an effort to squelch the need by engaging in physical activity. This entry has repeatedly appeared at various points in the stages. This is as a result of its high level of effectiveness. It will also prevent you from putting on extra weight while doing it. Furthermore, leading an active lifestyle is healthful.

*) Try your hardest to feel less stressed. Become positive in attitude. Take a nap or go to sleep as needed. Take some time to pamper yourself and de-stress.

Remaining a non-smoker or having recently made the decision to stop smoking, constantly keep in mind that the difficulties you encounter are pretty standard. Accept these difficulties since they provide a genuine significance to the overall experience.

Research has indicated that those who possess a high degree of confidence that giving up smoking will be easy typically succeed in doing so and maintaining their stopping habit. People who have self-doubt ultimately revert to their previous behaviour.

Recall that choosing to give up smoking is already a success. Keep your previous efforts if you have come this far. But you know you can achieve more tremendous success if you have the right mindset.

www.ingramcontent.com/pod-product-compliance
Lightning Source LLC
Chambersburg PA
CBHW052205110526
44591CB00012B/2083